Remember Not to Forget

A MEMORY OF THE HOLOCAUST

by Norman H. Finkelstein

illustrations by Lois and Lars Hokanson

 Franklin Watts New York/London/Toronto/Sydney 1985

Library of Congress Cataloging in Publication Data

Finkelstein, Norman H.
    Remember not to forget.

    Summary: A brief introduction to the Holocaust, in
which six million Jews were systematically exterminated
by the Nazis during World War II.
    1. Holocaust, Jewish (1939-1945)—Juvenile literature.
[1. Holocaust, Jewish (1939-1945)] I. Hokanson, Lois, ill.
II. Hokanson, Lars, ill.   III. Title.
D810.J4F46 1985 940.53'15'03924 84-17315
ISBN 0-531-04892-6

To Rosalind, with love
To Jeffrey, Robert and Risa, with hope

Jerusalem, Israel. It is spring, and visitors of all
faiths, from many countries, have come to this holy city
to celebrate Easter and Passover. A tall, handsome man
enters a crowded souvenir store on Jaffa Road. "You
speak German, perhaps?" the man asks the elderly shopkeeper.

"Yes, I do. Welcome to my store. You are enjoying
your visit to our country?" the old man responds in
flawless German.

"Yes, very much," the visitor answers. "Do you have
one of those Jewish candelabras—you know, the kind
that is the symbol of your country? I would like to take
one home as a remembrance of my visit."

"Oh," replies the shopkeeper, "you mean a Menorah. Yes, of course, let me show you some."

After the young German selects a Menorah and pays for it, the shopkeeper shakes his hand and wishes him a safe journey home. As the old man stretches his hand forward, a distinctive purple number can be seen tattooed on his arm. It is the sign of a person once marked for death by other Germans, not so long ago.

Between 1933 and 1945 six million Jewish men, women and children were murdered in Germany and other European countries. Although most of them died during World War II, they did not die because they were soldiers in battle. Neither were they guilty of any crimes. They died for only one reason: they were Jewish.

How could such a thing have happened? To answer this question, we must look far back in history.

Two thousand years ago the Jewish people lived in their own land. In the year 70 A.D. Jerusalem, their capital, was attacked and destroyed and the Jews were forced to leave their homes and their country.

For the next two thousand years they lived as wanderers and strangers in many countries of the world. And over those centuries the world witnessed the development of a new disease called anti-Semitism. Anti-Semitism means a hatred of Jewish people, their religion, and their culture.

Its causes are fear and lack of understanding.

Its symptoms are name calling, unfair treatment, and violence.

Even when the disease of anti-Semitism seems cured, the symptoms could break out again at any time.

As strangers in the countries where they lived, Jews were easy targets to blame for almost anything that might go wrong. Disease, hunger, war, unemployment—all these problems were blamed on the Jews.

For all those two thousand years Jews prayed for peace and the right to live again in freedom.

On the outside they endured:
Loneliness
Fear
Hate

On the inside they comforted themselves through:
Pride
Tradition
Religion

From 1933 to 1945 anti-Semitism was the official
law of the land in Germany and the countries of Europe
that Germany conquered. Under the slogan "The Jews
Are Our Misfortune," Adolf Hitler and his Nazi party
planned a series of programs designed to end what they
called "The Jewish Problem."

First came the humiliations and expulsions.

Jews were no longer citizens. Their businesses were
boycotted, and they were not allowed to practice their
professions or trades. Jewish children could no longer
attend public schools. And all Jews were forced to wear a
symbolic yellow star in public.

Jews had lived in Germany for hundreds of years and had become active participants in all aspects of society. Soldiers, lawyers, businessmen, teachers—they proudly considered themselves, first and foremost, citizens of Germany.

Yet, there had always been anti-Semitism in the background. So when the Nazis came to power, openly threatening Jews, the Jews could not at first believe that any actual harm would come to them. When anti-Jewish laws appeared, some Jews saw the danger signs and fled Germany. But many others waited. By the time the danger became real, it was too late for them to escape.

After the humiliations came increasing violence against Jews and Jewish property.

In 1938, in a two-day period in November, 30,000 Jews were arrested, and synagogues, Jewish institutions and businesses were destroyed. This time was called "Kristallnacht" or "crystal night" because of all the broken glass left on the streets of Germany. The same kind of violence was repeated throughout Europe as the Nazi armies marched from country to country.

But discrimination and violence were only the beginning; ghettos and concentration camps followed soon after.

The Nazis established a series of prison towns called concentration camps where people who were declared "enemies of the state" were sent. Just being Jewish was enough to put a person in a camp such as Buchenwald, Auschwitz or Treblinka.

To make life even more desperate, the Nazis forced Jews from their home towns and villages into special sections of larger towns and cities, which were surrounded by fences, walls, and armed soldiers. These guarded areas were called ghettos. There, in crowded, unsanitary conditions, the Jews tried to keep themselves and their dignity alive.

In the end, those who did not die of hunger or disease in the ghettos were doomed to death in the concentration camps, which became the killing places for six million Jews and millions of other innocent victims of the Nazis.

Few escaped.

It did not matter if you were rich or poor, young or old, religious or non-believing, ignorant or educated—if you were Jewish, you were marked for death.

As the Nazis overran the countries of Europe, special army troops rounded up Jewish residents, led them to woods or ditches and shot them in cold blood. Later, not satisfied with the speed of the killings, the Nazis introduced the use of poison gas, and enlarged the size of the concentration camps to receive increasing numbers of Jews from throughout Europe. In effect, they established a system unheard of in the whole history of the human race—a vast and precise killing business designed especially to destroy an entire people.

When World War II ended, over two-thirds of the Jews of Europe were dead, and the shocked world could only wonder how such a terrible event could have happened. It was an unimaginable tragedy, horrible and unbelievable; it was a savage firestorm of raging intensity— a Holocaust.

Some people believe that the passage of time has a way of healing sorrow. In the long history of the Jewish people there have been many sorrowful events. While the span of centuries may dull some of the original pain, Jews have never allowed the memory of these earlier tragedies to be erased. In the same way, they will never forget the Holocaust.

In 1948 the state of Israel was born. After two thousand years the Jewish people had their own land again. Many of those who came home to Israel were survivors of the Holocaust. Although they personally carried the deep scars of suffering, other Jews throughout the world shared their sadness.

Sometimes it is hard to express your innermost feelings to others. You want to spare the ones you love from suffering, pain, and embarrassment. The tragedy of the Holocaust was so great that some people didn't want to talk about it or even remind themselves of their experiences during those tragic years.

But other people saw the need to keep the memory of the Holocaust alive in order to prevent such a catastrophe from happening again. Especially within the last ten years, the subject of the Holocaust has been introduced in schools and universities. Many books and magazine articles have been written, and films and television programs have been produced which portray many people's experiences of the Holocaust.

In 1953, through a special law passed by the Israeli parliament, the Knesset, a national institution called Yad Vashem was established to study and research the Holocaust.

The major task of Yad Vashem is to document all the events of the Holocaust, especially the brave fight for life demonstrated by Jews all over Europe. The archives and library of Yad Vashem contain the actual records of the futile struggle for life waged by millions of Jewish men, women and children. Outside, a lovely tree-lined path honors those non-Jews of Europe who risked their own lives to save their Jewish neighbors.

Since the end of World War II, there have been a variety of events and programs honoring the dead. The one thing that was lacking was a standard way or date to recognize the importance of the Holocaust and honor the memory of the millions of people who died.

In 1959 the Israeli Knesset passed another special law creating *Yom Hashoa*, Holocaust Remembrance Day, to be observed each year on the 27th day of the month of Nisan, according to the Jewish calendar. This date coincides with the beginning of the heroic revolt against the Nazis by Jews in the Warsaw Ghetto in 1943. It usually occurs in April.

The rest of the Jewish world has taken the lead from Israel and now, each year, throughout the world,

Jewish communities observe that date to honor the memory of six million Jewish dead.

The way in which this day is observed varies from one community to another. In Israel, a national program is held in the large courtyard at Yad Vashem. Also, at eight o'clock in the morning, air-raid sirens wail, and all over Israel, normal everyday activity comes to a complete stop. Two minutes of silence are observed as a tribute to those who died.

In other countries, including the United States, the day is marked by special meetings and religious services. These may be large, outdoor programs for the whole community or simple gatherings in local temples. Holocaust survivors are often featured participants.

As the years pass, however, those who were actual survivors of the Nazi brutality grow older and die. Soon there will be no one left alive who personally lived through the Holocaust. So, it becomes even more important to remember those terrible years and how they began, and to remember how cruelty, hatred and discrimination led to violence, death and destruction.

On *Yom Hashoa* Jews around the world will pause each year to remember . . . to remember not to forget.

ABOUT THE AUTHOR

Norman H. Finkelstein, a graduate of Hebrew College and Boston University, is a public school librarian. He is also an instructor at Hebrew College of Boston and has taught religious studies in several Jewish religious schools in the Boston area.

A former member of the Board of Directors of the Massachusetts Association for Educational Media, Mr. Finkelstein has published articles in professional media journals. *Remember Not To Forget*, Mr. Finkelstein's first book for children, earned him the 1984 Holzman Award from Hebrew College—an award presented annually in recognition of creative new materials for Jewish education.

Mr. Finkelstein lives in Framingham, Massachusetts, with his wife and their three children.

ABOUT THE ARTISTS

Lois and Lars Hokanson, who specialize in woodcut illustrations, worked for ten years as free-lance designers and illustrators in London, England. They have recently relocated their studio to Lancaster, Pennsylvania, where they now live with their two children.

CHILDREN'S ROOM

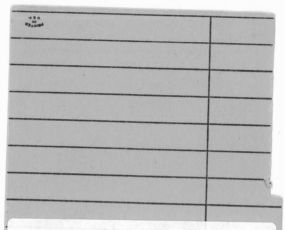

DEMCO